SUPER
LITTLE GIANT BOOK™ OF
WEIRD ANIMAL FACTS

SUPER
LITTLE GIANT BOOK™ OF
WEIRD ANIMAL FACTS

THE DIAGRAM GROUP

Sterling Publishing Co., Inc.
New York

Library of Congress Cataloging-in-Publication Data Available

10 9 8 7 6 5 4 3 2 1

Published in 2005 by Sterling Publishing Co., Inc.
387 Park Avenue South, New York, N.Y. 10016

Created by Diagram Visual Information Limited
195 Kentish Town Road, London, NW5 2JU, England

© 2005 Diagram Visual Information Limited

Distributed in Canada by Sterling Publishing
c/o Canadian Manda Group, 165 Dufferin Street
Toronto, Ontario, Canada M6K 3H6

Written by	The Diagram Group
Production	Richard Hummerstone
Art direction	Anthony Atherton, Darren Bennett
Picture research	Neil McKenna
Artists	Pavel Kostal, Kathy McDougall,
	Coral Mula, Graham Rosewarne

Printed in China
All rights reserved

ISBN 1-4027-2596-5

For information about custom editions, special sales, premium and
corporate purchases, please contact Sterling Special Sales
Department at 800-805-5489 or specialsales@sterlingpub.com.

INTRODUCTION

It takes all creatures great and small to make up the world:

* If a cockroach loses its head, it can continue to live for more than a week before starving to death!

* With enough venom to kill 100 people, the poison-arrow frog is the world's most poisonous creature!

* Female octopuses can be up to 40,000 times heavier than their male mates!

* Deep in the oceanic abyss, lantern fish attract prey with built-in headlights!

* A bald eagle's nest can be nine feet across and weigh as much as a large automobile!

* Komodo dragons smell through their tongues!

* Sea cucumbers sacrifice their own guts to escape predators!

* Archerfish can shoot insects down with water for them to eat!

* Tapeworms can grow to 50 feet long inside a human intestine, and don't need a mate to reproduce!

Welcome to the world of
WEIRD CREATURES!

CONTENTS

12 Population explosion
13 Snappy monsters
14 Misplaced
16 A spider bigger than your hand
18 Long life
19 Drunk on cherries
20 Eyes can see you
22 Name of a dog
23 Not a piggy
24 Headless
25 The Devil's creature?
26 On your head for life
28 Can you dig it?
29 Eyes bigger than its stomach
30 Mind the lines
31 Wandering albatross
32 Awesome claw
33 Lucky for some
34 In a flap
35 Hairy animal
36 Deadly thread
37 Birdbath
38 Watch where you step!
39 Pet monster
40 Moon madness
42 Dog talk
44 Giant lobsters
45 Power poisoner
46 White elephant
47 Pond skating
48 Not a fox
49 Good dad
50 Standing tall
51 Star nose
52 Inside out
53 Roadrunner
54 Cockroach cure
55 Mighty biter
56 Big girls
57 Strange cousins
58 Many millions

59	Getting the hump	84	Worms for later
60	Bird bell	85	Big mouth
61	Sshhhhhhhh!	86	Water walker
62	Shaggy yak	87	Misnomer
63	Floating shell	88	Stinking spit
64	Monster mouth	89	Turned turtle
65	Food for thought	90	Enormous nest
66	Lobster lines	92	Money bird
67	Flying snakes!	93	Flying spiders
68	Loud howler	94	Dressed crabs
70	Summer holidays	95	Bad mother
72	A is for aardvark	96	To bee or not to bee?
73	Bird planters	97	Hopeful mothers
74	Headlamps	98	Anting
75	Tree tunnels	99	Killer fleas
76	Dragonfish	100	It's just not cricket!
77	Huge horns	102	Big bad toad
78	A flea on a bee	103	Gulp
79	Tiny tots actual size	104	Flea food
80	Beavering away	105	Cuttlefish
82	Toothless terror	106	Tail leap
83	Creature comforts	107	Tail light

107 Jerboa
108 Spot the worm
109 Dead? Or not?
110 Amber trap
111 Cleaning service
112 Bubbling under
114 Spider monkey
115 Ancient crab
116 Water bears
116 Black and white
118 Going down
120 Big beak
121 Wall walker
122 No nose
123 Tiny flier
124 Sea horse tails
125 Tremendous teeth
126 Who am I?
128 Walking on water
129 Being right can get
you into trouble
130 Expanding ribs

132 A long way home
134 Hot wings
136 Long distance
traveler
137 Sensing sound
138 Sea spider
139 Fine feelers
140 Echidna kids
141 Skin-eaters in
your bed!
142 Tongue twister
143 Mmm yummy!
144 Land or sea
144 Stinging tale
146 Advancing from
the rear
147 Mouth in the middle
148 A taste for blood
149 Tasting the air
150 Startling eyes
151 Night birth
152 Handwalking

153 Flying fish
154 Magic uses of bats
155 Bad-luck bats
156 A cackle of hyenas
157 Floating food
158 Built for speed
159 Web-footed dog
160 Fossil flatulence
161 A lot of guts
162 Big bug
163 Portuguese
    man-of-war
164 Blindfold bat
165 Busy mother
166 Big bad wolf?
167 Sniffing beaks
168 Elephant ears
169 On its back
170 Sea cows
172 Helpful hands
172 Big bite
174 Sick as a fly

176 One is better
    than none
177 Returning home
178 Soaring
180 Camouflage
182 Optical illusion
183 Hunting machine
184 Spitting fish
185 Sleeping your
    life away
186 Coral jungle
187 Wingless flier
188 Fangs a lot!
189 Pleased to meet you!
189 Boing!!
190 A love dance
191 Food for thought
192 Moth facts
194 Island poisoner
195 Climbing crabs
196 Taking off
197 Buried alive

198 R-U-C-reus?
199 Hello, I must be going!
200 Steady as she goes
202 Outnumbered
203 Feeding on the wing
204 Switched on
205 Friendly foe
206 A meal on a stick
207 Flying lizard
208 A rat as big as a cat!
208 Tongue-tied
210 Furry bees
212 Ready to go
213 Fancy a bite?
214 Fastest creature
215 Big burrower
216 It's the pits
217 Short life
218 Jawless sucker
220 Food on the wing
222 Ant herders

222 Rhino horn
224 Bandicoot babies
225 Backing into home
226 Eyes alert
228 Sea squirt
229 High pantry
230 Breathing through your stomach
232 Hello buddy
234 The eyes have it
236 Sweet talk
238 Sidewinder
238 Night light
240 No-eared earwig
241 Birds with teeth
241 Mouthful
242 Small but deadly
243 Leaps and bounds
244 Plant animals
244 Amazing ants
245 Loads of legs
246 Brave dentist

246 Termite towers
247 Don't bee-lieve your eyes
248 Titanic tongue
250 A cracking story
250 Clam up!
251 That's cool
252 What's the point?
253 Lipsmackin'
254 White lie
255 Insect ID
256 Still swimming
257 Snail's pace
258 Enormous eggs
258 Big croc
260 Flying fish
261 Multicolored marvel
262 Pink plumage
262 Keep moving
263 Heavy house
264 Slow sloth
265 Fearsome fish

266 Hook head
268 Dancing bees
269 Counting sheep
270 World-wide web
271 Quick ears
272 Bugs weigh in top
273 Lucky donkey
274 Seeking a partner
275 American football
276 Bees never tell lies
277 Albatross forecast
278 Perfect pitch
279 Tunnel vision
280 A fish out of water
282 Counting feathers
283 Swan song
284 Snakes' sense
285 Rat tales
286 Index

11

POPULATION

EXPLOSION

Inside your body
there live millions of bacteria—
tiny cells you have swallowed.
Most can reproduce themselves
every 15 minutes, so in 24
hours one bacterium can
produce

4,000,000,000,000

new cells. There are
probably more bacteria
living in your mouth
now than the total
number of all the human
beings who have ever
lived.

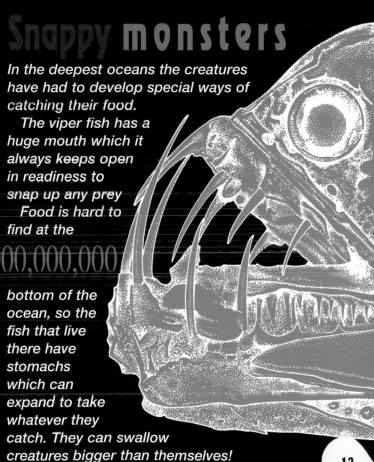

Snappy monsters

In the deepest oceans the creatures have had to develop special ways of catching their food.

The viper fish has a huge mouth which it always keeps open in readiness to snap up any prey

Food is hard to find at the

000,000,000

bottom of the ocean, so the fish that live there have stomachs which can expand to take whatever they catch. They can swallow creatures bigger than themselves!

Misplaced

Can you see a fish in this picture?
In it there is a plaice—a European
flounder. Some fish are able to
change the patterns and color of
their skins to match the seafloor on
which they lie.

Here he is without
the surrounding seabed.

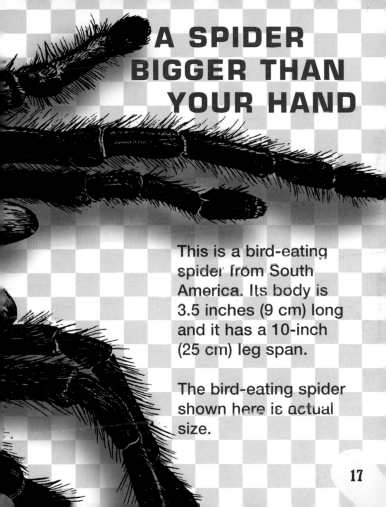

A SPIDER BIGGER THAN YOUR HAND

This is a bird-eating spider from South America. Its body is 3.5 inches (9 cm) long and it has a 10-inch (25 cm) leg span.

The bird-eating spider shown here is actual size.

Long life

The oldest recorded tortoise was 152 years old—that is twice the average human life span.

Drunk on cherries

When fruit gets overripe, the juice can turn into a kind of alcohol. Some fruit-eating birds have been known to eat overripe cherries and get slightly drunk.

Eyes can see you

In each compound eye, a fly
has at least 4,000 different lenses.
In some species almost all of the
head is made up of

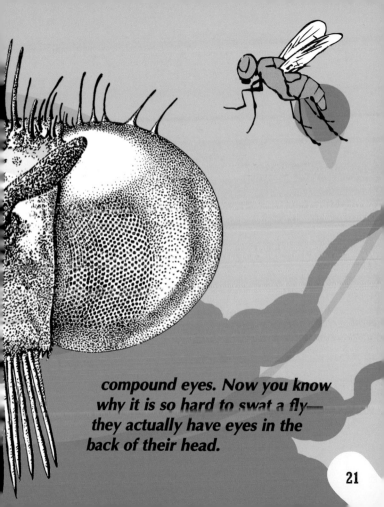

compound eyes. Now you know why it is so hard to swat a fly— they actually have eyes in the back of their head.

Name of a dog

A tax collector, called Ludwig Dobermann, lived in Germany about 120 years ago. He was not welcome when he came for money. To protect him, he bred fierce large dogs. They became known as Doberman pinschers and are still used as guard dogs today.

Not a piggy

Tapirs, which live in Central and South America and Malaysia, look a little like pigs.

But they do not belong to the pig family. Only about 3 feet (91 cm) tall, they are related to horses and rhinos.

HEADLESS

A cockroach can
live for more than
a week without
its head.

After that,
it starves
to death.

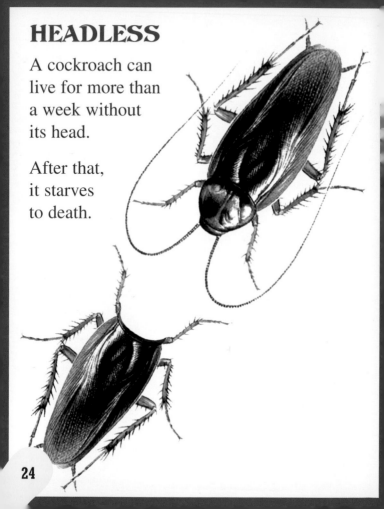

The Devil's creature?

Goats have been linked to the Devil for a very long time. One superstition says that it is impossible to watch a goat for a whole day because it will always slip away for a few minutes to meet the Devil.

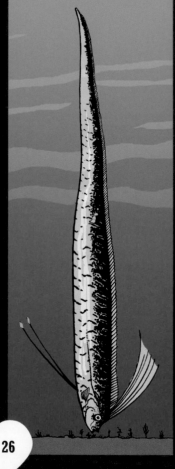

ON YOUR

When you get that sinking feeling, think of the poor old oarfish. One of nature's most mysterious creatures, it lives at depths of 1,000 to 2,000 feet (300–600 m) in

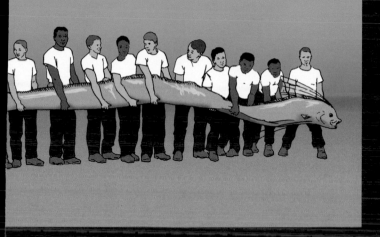

HEAD FOR LIFE

oceans all over the world. Its main food is krill: tiny creatures that it finds in deep mud at the bottom of the ocean. The oarfish is so determined to find food that it lives its whole life floating head-down. Oarfish as long as 49 feet (15 m) have been found washed up on beaches. An 11.5 feet (3.5 m) long oarfish was caught using an ordinary fishing rod at Cleveland, England in February 2003.

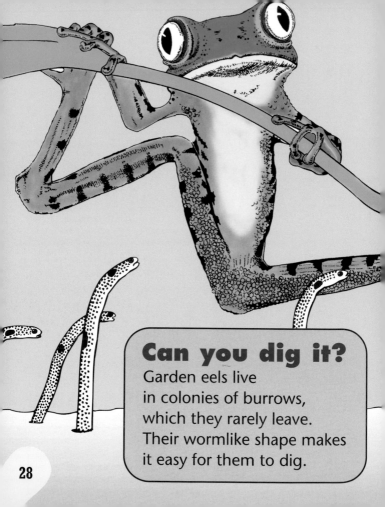

Can you dig it?

Garden eels live
in colonies of burrows,
which they rarely leave.
Their wormlike shape makes
it easy for them to dig.

28

EYES BIGGER THAN ITS STOMACH

The bug-eyed tree frog uses its eyes to eat with. When they swallow they close their eyelids, press down with their very tough eyeballs, and lower the roof of their mouth against their tongue. This forces the food down and into their stomach.

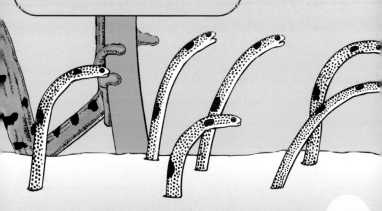

Mind the lines

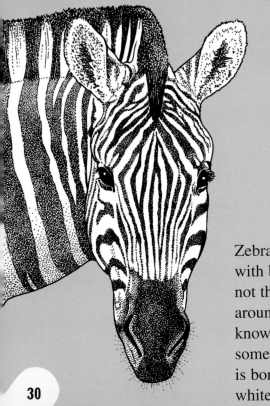

Zebras are white
with black stripes,
not the other way
around. Scientists
know this because
sometimes a zebra
is born with
white stripes.

Wandering albatross

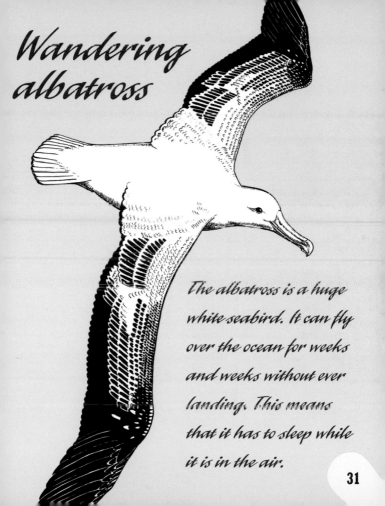

The albatross is a huge white seabird. It can fly over the ocean for weeks and weeks without ever landing. This means that it has to sleep while it is in the air.

Awesome claw

Male fiddler crabs have just one giant claw.
They use it to show off to female fiddler crabs.

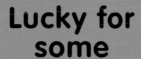

Lucky for some

Black cats are lucky in Britain, but unlucky in America.

In a flap

Insects have to beat their wings very fast to keep their bodies in the air. The hawk moth beats its wings 5,400 times in one minute. Honey bees do 7,800 flaps a minute, and tiny midges do it 60,000 times a minute.

Hairy **animal**

The sea otter needs to keep warm in cold water, so it has developed a fur coat of millions of small body hairs.

In an area as big as this stamp it has 450,000 hairs!

Deadly thread

A bolas spider uses
a thread with a sticky ball of
silk at the end to catch insects.
The weight of the ball winds the
thread around the prey so that it
cannot escape.

Birdbath

Some birds have a bath in water, but others use dirt! They cover themselves with dust and shake it through their feathers. The dust helps to get rid of lice.

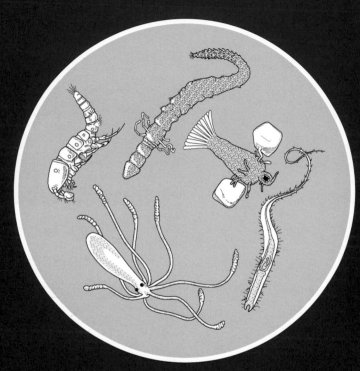

Watch where you step!

When you walk on the beach, there are millions of tiny creatures—meiofauna—under your feet. They live in the spaces between the grains of sand.

Pet monster

The hellbender is a giant salamander that can be 30 inches (76 cm) long. When kept as a pet, it will eat dogfood.

Moon madness

There are lots of legends and stories about wolves. The most terrifying tales are about werewolves—human beings that turn into savage wolves when the Moon is full.

Dog talk

Dogs can
only make
ten different
vocal sounds.
Cats can
manage
about 100.

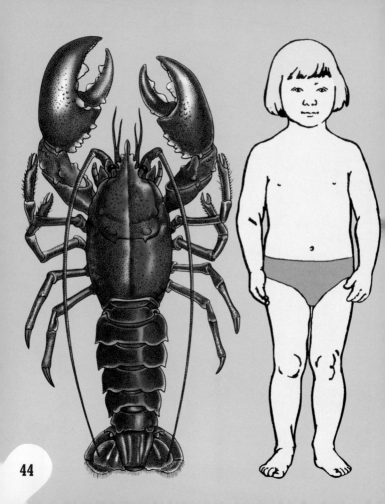

GIANT **LOBSTERS**

The average height of a girl at the age of three is 37 inches (94 cm), less than an inch (2.5 cm) more than some monster American lobsters that measure 36 inches (91 cm) from the end of the tail to the tip of the claws.

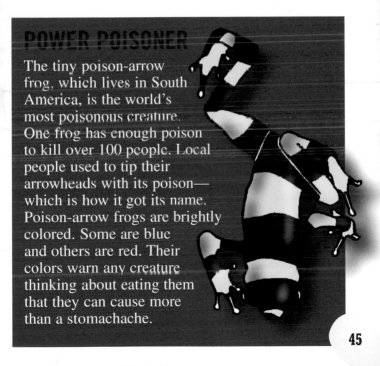

POWER POISONER

The tiny poison-arrow frog, which lives in South America, is the world's most poisonous creature. One frog has enough poison to kill over 100 people. Local people used to tip their arrowheads with its poison—which is how it got its name. Poison-arrow frogs are brightly colored. Some are blue and others are red. Their colors warn any creature thinking about eating them that they can cause more than a stomachache.

White elephant

The expression "a white elephant" means something that it is expensive or beautiful but useless. It came from Siam (now Thailand), where white elephants were very rare and were not made to work.

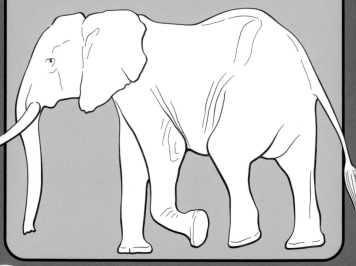

Pond skating

Pond skaters can walk on water.
Their long legs and feet spread their
weight out so that they don't sink.

Not a fox

The flying fox is actually a bat. Unlike other bats, it eats fruit and has good eyesight.

Good dad

A king penguin chick takes 60 days to hatch
out of its egg. During this time, the male
penguin stands on the Antarctic ice,
cradling the egg on its feet and keeping
it warm under a flap of soft feathers.

49

Standing tall

This is a gerenuk antelope, that has specialized in browsing bushes for food. It can stand on its back legs for long periods of time.

Star nose

The star-nosed mole uses the tentacles around its nose to help find food. It lives underground but spends a lot of time underwater in murky ponds snuffling around in the mud.

Inside out

The crown of thorns starfish turns its stomach inside out over coral polyps to digest them, turning large areas of coral reef into bleached white skeletons.

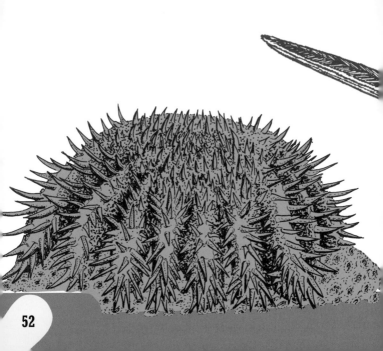

Roadrunner

The roadrunner is a bird that eats snakes. It chases them across the desert at 25 miles per hour (40 kph) until they are too tired to fight back.

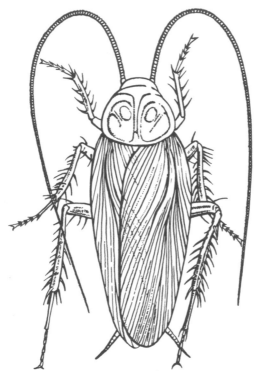

Cockroach cure

Some ancient Greeks believed that you could cure an earache by stuffing cockroach stomachs in your ear.

The king cobra bites more people every year than any other snake. It can even kill an elephant.

Mighty biter

55

Big girls

In many species the males and females are different sizes. For example, men are usually taller and bigger than women. The blanket octopus is an extreme example of this. The male blanket octopus is a tiny creature about an inch (2.5 cm) long. The female blanket octopus is 6 feet (1.8 m) long and 40,000 times heavier! Male blanket octopuses never argue with their wives.

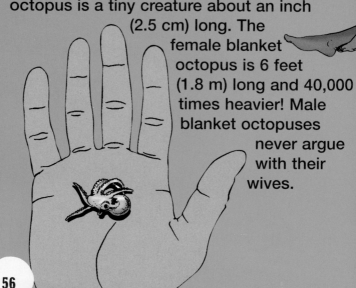

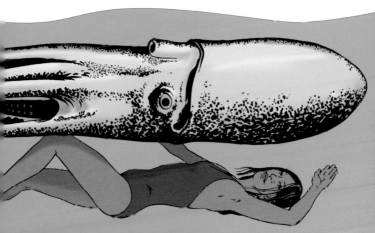

STRANGE COUSINS

The common garden snail is related to octopuses and giant squids. They are all mollusks. Mollusks are creatures with soft bodies and no bones. Fortunately, giant squids never come round to your garden to eat your cabbages!

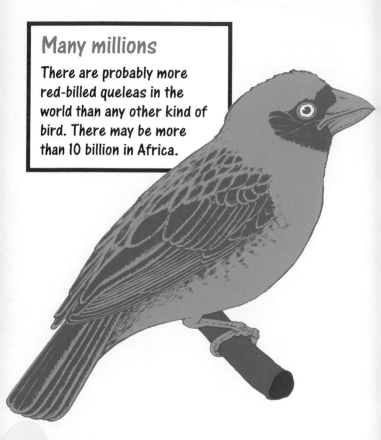

Many millions

There are probably more red-billed queleas in the world than any other kind of bird. There may be more than 10 billion in Africa.

Getting the hump

There are two types of camel. A dromedary has one hump so its back looks like a **D** on its side. A Bactrian camel has two humps so its back looks like a **B** on its side.

Bird bell

The male bellbird is one of the loudest birds. Sounding like a clanging bell, it can be heard over half a mile (800 m) away. It sings to attract a mate. When a female comes, it dances out and sings again.

Sshhhhhhhh!

Bushbabies hunt for food at night. They have such good hearing that when they sleep during the day, they fold up their ears to cover their ear holes. This stops the noises of the forest from waking them up.

Shaggy yak

The wild yak lives high up in the Himalayan mountains.
It has a shaggy coat that can keep it warm in
temperatures as low as −40°F (−40°C).

Floating shell

The pearly nautilus is the last surviving member of a group of sea creatures that filled the oceans millions of years ago. Its shell has many gas-filled chambers that help it to float at the right depth.

Monster
MOUTH

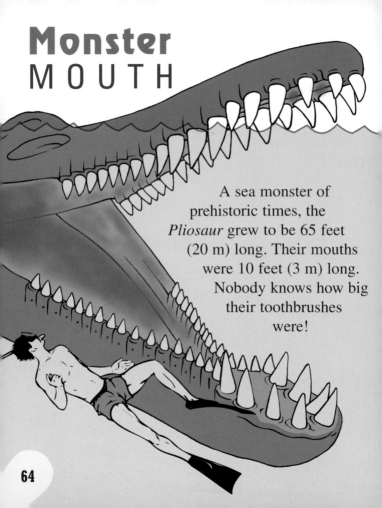

A sea monster of prehistoric times, the *Pliosaur* grew to be 65 feet (20 m) long. Their mouths were 10 feet (3 m) long. Nobody knows how big their toothbrushes were!

Food for thought

In 1957 a swarm of thousands of millions of locusts ate crops that could have fed one million people for a whole year.

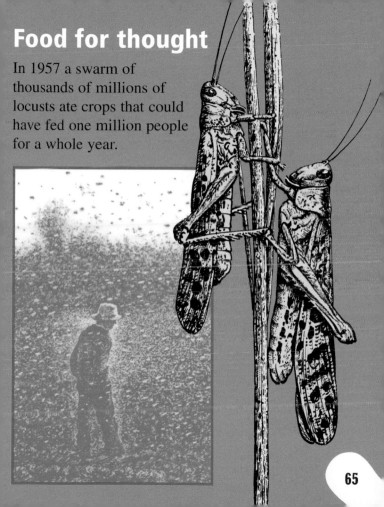

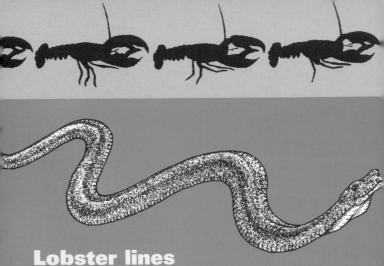

Lobster lines

At the end of each summer, spiny lobsters move from their homes to get away from great sea storms. They line up in long columns on the ocean bed and march off together to find somewhere safe.

Flying snakes!

Some snakes can fly. The flying snake launches itself from a branch and then flattens its body so that it acts like a parachute.

Loud howler

Howler monkeys live in the forests of
South America. They get together
in groups and howl so loudly that
they can be heard 2 miles
(3.2 km) away.

SUMMER
HOLIDAYS

As winter approaches in North America the
monarch butterfly flies south to Mexico.
It averages 80 miles (130 km) a day, traveling
over 1,800 miles (2,900 km). When they arrive in
Mexico, they cluster together to form large towers
of fluttering butterflies.

A is for aardvark

Aardvarks are very unusual animals. They have eyes like a deer, ears like a rabbit, a nose like a pig and a tail like a rat. It also has a long, sticky tongue which it uses to eat ants.

Bird planters

Thick-billed nutcracker birds hide stores of nuts to eat during the winter. A bird usually remembers where it buried the nuts, but it sometimes misses a few. These grow into trees, helping the forest to spread.

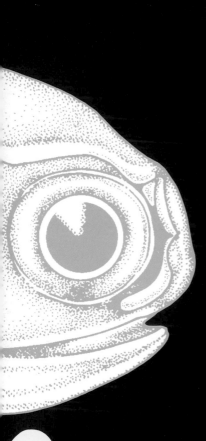

Headlamps

In the black depths of the ocean, eyes have nothing to see most of the time. The *Diaphus*, a lantern fish, has had to adapt by making its own light. In this case the head of the fish illuminates the way, like an automobile's headlamps.

Tree tunnels

Some weaver birds build very unusual nests. The nest is made of reeds and has a long tunnel that leads to the entrance. This stops other creatures from getting in and eating their eggs.

Dragonfish

The dragonfish might look beautiful, but it can be dangerous. The spikes sticking out of its body have poisoned tips.

Huge horns

The male moose has the biggest antlers of any deer. They can grow up to 6 feet (1.8 m) wide.

A FLEA ON A BEE

A queen bee is only 0.6 inches (15 mm) long, but even smaller creatures live on it. Here is the leg of a bee magnified ten times and below is the tiny flea that lives on the bee.

It's smaller than a grain of salt. The flea is magnified 100 times.

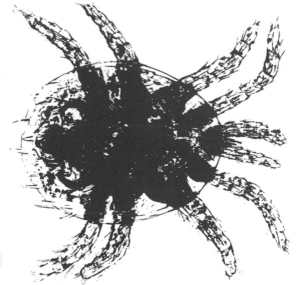

TINY TOTS *ACTUAL SIZE*

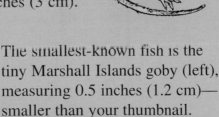

The smallest bird in the world, shown here actual size (left), is Helena's hummingbird from Cuba. An average adult male measures only 2.25 inches (5.7 cm) from the tip of its beak to the tip of its tail.

Drawn actual size (right), the pygmy shrew has a head and body length of 1.7 inches (4.3 cm). Its tail adds another 1.2 inches (3 cm).

The smallest-known fish is the tiny Marshall Islands goby (left), measuring 0.5 inches (1.2 cm)—smaller than your thumbnail.

Beavering away

Beavers can cut up a log 20 inches (82 cm) thick with their sharp teeth in just 15 minutes. They cut down trees to make a dam and then build their home, called a lodge, in the pond which forms behind the dam.

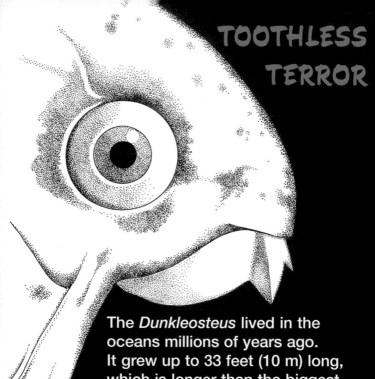

TOOTHLESS TERROR

The *Dunkleosteus* lived in the oceans millions of years ago. It grew up to 33 feet (10 m) long, which is longer than the biggest sharks today.

Creature comforts

Orangutans build nests. Every night they make themselves a comfortable mattress of branches and leaves high up in the trees.

Worms for later

The mole catches worms to eat.
If it has too many, it bites the
worms on the back to stop them
moving and keeps them for later.

Big mouth

A pelican can hold more in its beak than in its belly.

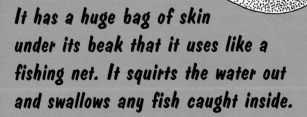

It has a huge bag of skin under its beak that it uses like a fishing net. It squirts the water out and swallows any fish caught inside.

Water walker

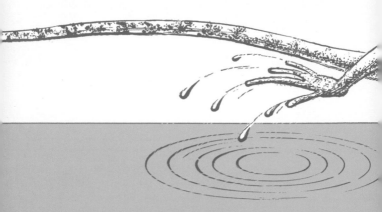

One South American lizard can walk on water. If it needs to escape, it runs as fast as it can across the nearest pond. It has very wide toes and feet that stop it from sinking.

Misnomer

A silverfish is not made of silver and is not a fish. It is a tiny insect that lives in houses, eating anything with glue on it.

Stinking spit

Fulmars protect their nests by spitting an oil at any predator that comes near. The oil is made in the bird's stomach from the food it eats, and it smells terrible.

Turned turtle

A female green turtle
lays an average of 1,800
eggs in her life. Of these,
1,395 don't hatch, 374
hatch but quickly die, and
only three live long
enough to breed.

Enormous nest

Bald eagles build the world's biggest nests. Each year the eagles use the same nest, adding more branches. A nest can be nine feet (2.7 m) across, 18 feet (5.5 m) high, and weigh as much as a large automobile.

Money bird

Male quetzal birds have beautiful long tail feathers which were once worn by Mayan chiefs as a royal symbol. Now the bird is the national symbol of Guatemala and the country's money is named after it.

Flying spiders

Spiders do not have wings, but some can fly!
They release a long thread of silk that catches
the wind and carries them high into the air.
Small spiders can travel for hundreds of miles
(km) in this way.

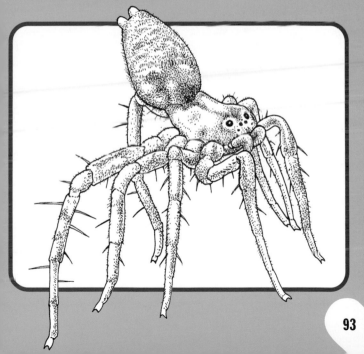

Dressed crabs

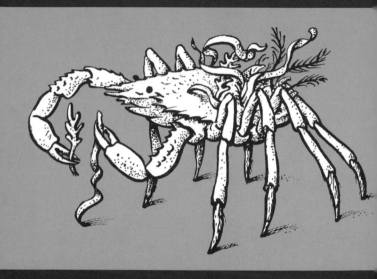

Spider crabs like dressing up in disguise so much they let other creatures build homes on their backs. These crabs are quite common but they are difficult to see because they look so much like the seabed.

Bad mother

A sow and her six piglets were sentenced to death for eating a child in France in 1547. The sow was killed but the piglets were allowed to live because of their youth and the bad example set by their mother.

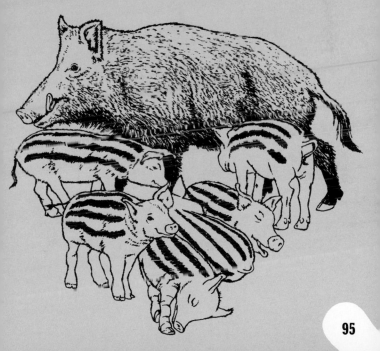

To bee or not to bee?

The flower of this orchid plant looks just like a bee. Other bees think it is a female and try to mate with it. Pollen gets stuck to them, which the bees then carry to other orchids.

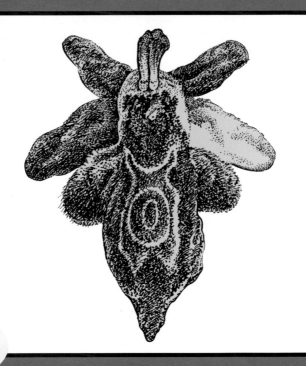

Hopeful mothers

The sunfish holds the record for producing the most eggs.

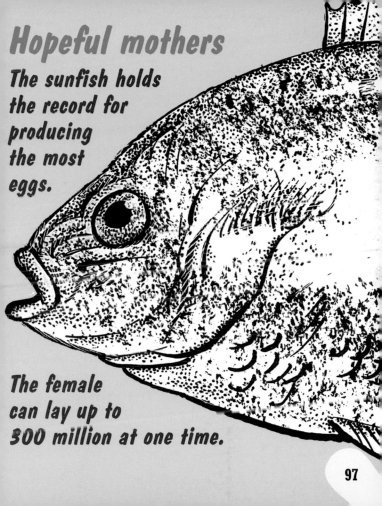

The female can lay up to 300 million at one time.

ANTING

Some birds use ants to clean themselves.
They sit with their feathers fluffed up and
let the ants crawl over them. The ants squirt
out an acid that kills mites living on the
birds' feathers.

Killer **fleas**

A deadly disease, called the bubonic plague, killed more than a quarter of all the people in Europe in the 14th century. The disease was spread from rats to humans by tiny biting fleas.

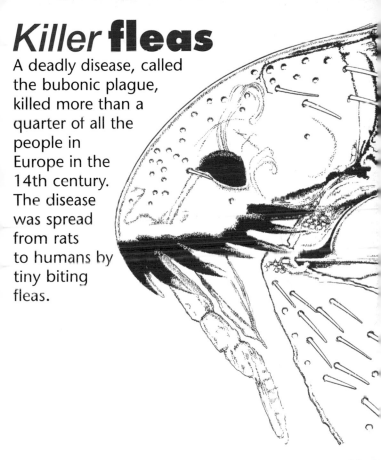

It's just not cricket!

The Sri Lankan cricket is one of many animals that tries to avoid being eaten by looking like something else—in its case, a leaf.

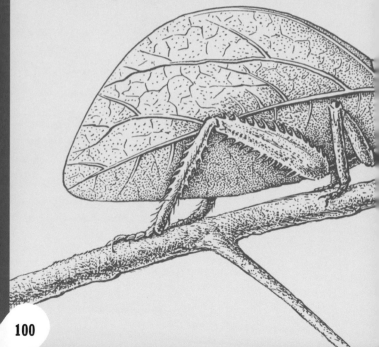

BIG BAD TOAD

Cane toads are big, ugly, and a terrible nuisance, especially in Australia where they eat everything in sight and make life very hard for other animals. They can also squirt poison at you from bulging sacs on their shoulders.

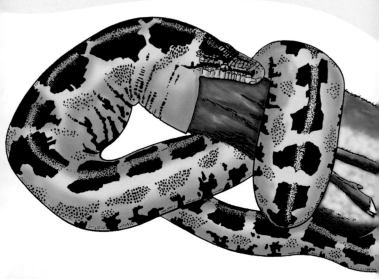

GULP

The reticulated python is a snake with no venom. It seizes and crushes its prey before swallowing it whole. Pythons can be 30 feet (9 m) long, so they can swallow animals as large as deer.

103

Flea food

There are about 1,800 different kinds of fleas in the world. They live on the blood of people, birds, and other animals. Most kinds of fleas prefer one type of animal but will feed on any blood if they are really hungry.

Cuttlefish

Cuttlefish are amazing sea creatures that can change color in the blink of an eye. They can flash red when they are angry, or turn sand-colored to hide on the seabed.

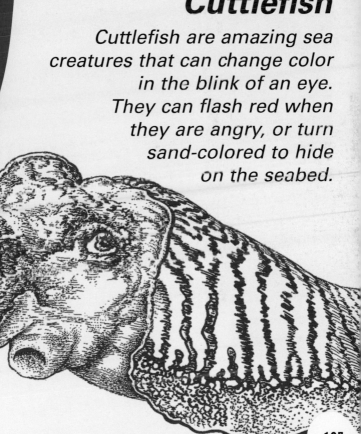

Tail leap

The average domestic cat can jump about five times as high as the length of its tail.

Tail light

The Australians use camels to carry goods over dry barren land. If traveling on roads, the camels avoid accidents with vehicles approaching from the rear by having lights attached to their tails called "tail lights."

Jerboa

The tiny jerboa lives in the desert and can jump around on its hind legs like a kangaroo. Its huge ears help to keep it cool.

107

Spot the worm

The African giant earthworm can grow up to 22 feet (6.7 m) long. If you placed one around the edge of a pool table it would cover all the pockets.

Dead? Or not?

A large American opossum plays dead when it is attacked. It lies still with its mouth open and eyes staring. Once the enemy has gone away it takes a quick look around and comes back to life.

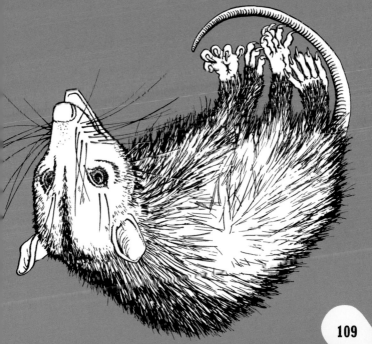

Amber trap

Some insects have been preserved for millions of years. They were trapped in the sap that oozed from trees. Over millions of years this sap has hardened into amber beads like glass, with the insects trapped inside for all time.

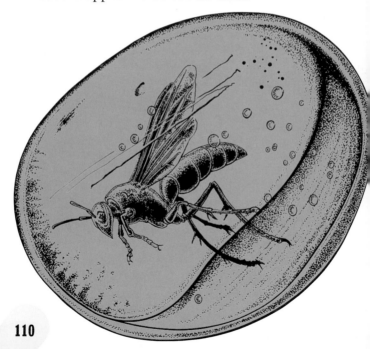

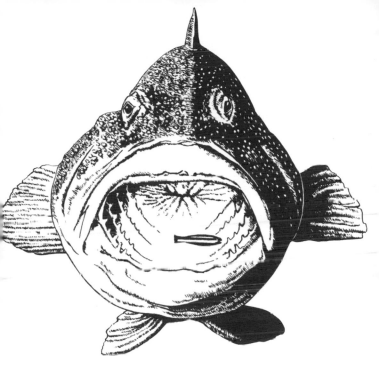

Cleaning service

Some wrasse fish specialize in cleaning
the mouths of other fish. The brave little
wrasse in this picture is collecting bits
of uneaten food from the huge mouth
of a grouper fish.

111

Bubbling under

Humpback whales catch fish in a net of bubbles. A whale swims under a shoal of fish and squirts out a circle of bubbles from its blowhole. The fish stay inside the circle, and the whale then swallows them.

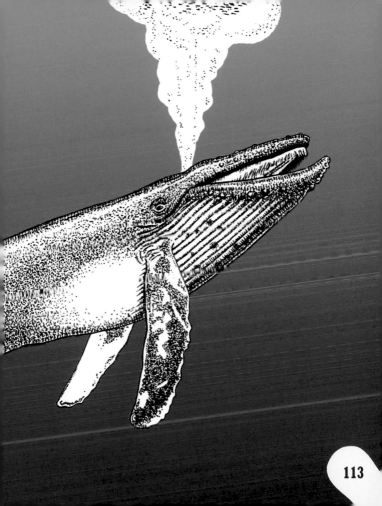

Spider monkey

Many South American monkeys have prehensile tails. That means their tails can grip things. The spider monkey uses its tail like an extra arm when it is climbing in the trees.

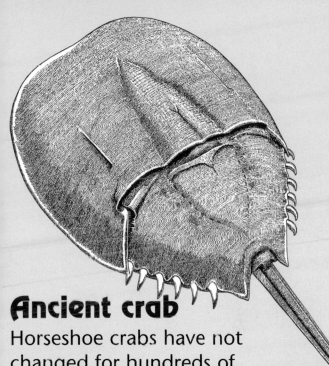

Ancient crab

Horseshoe crabs have not changed for hundreds of millions of years. They can have bodies as flat as they are because many of their organs are in their legs.

Water bears

Water bears are tiny creatures, but they are very tough. They can survive anywhere from tropical forests to the frozen Arctic. They are a bit like worms, except that they have legs, and are no bigger than the head of a pin.

Black and white

There are 16 species of penguin and they all have black-and-white feathers. Penguins cannot fly, but they are great swimmers. Their coloring makes them hard to spot when they are in the water. From above, their black backs blend into the dark water below. From below, their white bellies blend into the icy brightness above.

117

Going down

Sperm whales are the largest hunters on Earth. The biggest grow to 65 feet (19.8 m) and weigh 35 tons or more. They have long thin jaws lined with sharp teeth that are ideal for catching squid. Sperm whales can dive 6,500 feet (1,980 m) to find their favorite food—that's five times the height of the Empire State Building.

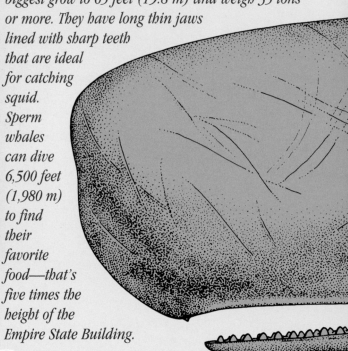

Big beak

Toucans have extremely large beaks.
They use them to reach fruit on branches
that are too thin to stand on.
Although it is big, a toucan's
beak is actually
very light.

Wall walker

Geckoes can easily walk up walls and across ceilings. Their feet have hundreds of tiny rough ridges that can grip surfaces as smooth as glass.

No nose

Salamanders probably look a lot like the very first creatures that lived on land. Most do not have lungs and breathe through their skin instead. Much of their time is spent doing nothing, hiding under stones or logs.

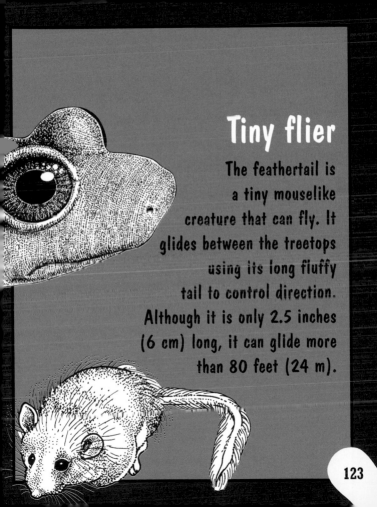

Tiny flier

The feathertail is a tiny mouselike creature that can fly. It glides between the treetops using its long fluffy tail to control direction. Although it is only 2.5 inches (6 cm) long, it can glide more than 80 feet (24 m).

Sea horse tails

Sea horses live among water weeds in the oceans. They have prehensile tails, rather like monkeys, which they use to hold on to weed stems.

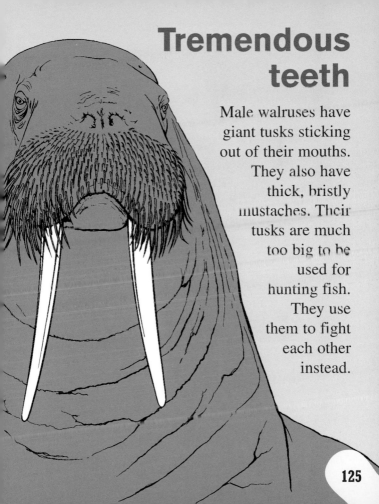

Tremendous teeth

Male walruses have giant tusks sticking out of their mouths. They also have thick, bristly mustaches. Their tusks are much too big to be used for hunting fish. They use them to fight each other instead.

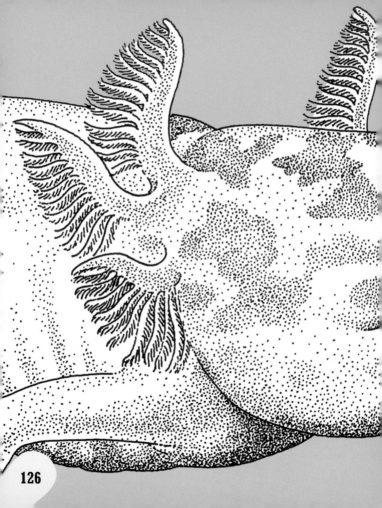

Who am I?

The axolotl normally lives underwater and breathes through gills like a fish. If the water gets too shallow though, it can gradually stop using its gills and start using its lungs to breathe instead.

Walking on water

The jacana
has huge feet
with very long
toes. These
feet mean
that this
waterbird
can walk

around on
floating leaves
without sinking.

128

an get you into trouble

The slow-moving
right whale got its name
because it was said to be the "right"
whale to hunt in the days when whales were
hunted from rowboats. So many were hunted
and killed that only a few survive today.

Expanding ribs

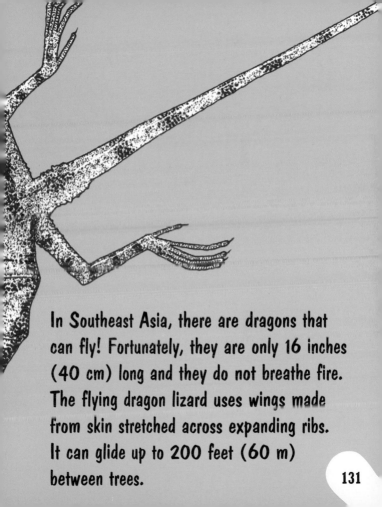

In Southeast Asia, there are dragons that can fly! Fortunately, they are only 16 inches (40 cm) long and they do not breathe fire. The flying dragon lizard uses wings made from skin stretched across expanding ribs. It can glide up to 200 feet (60 m) between trees.

131

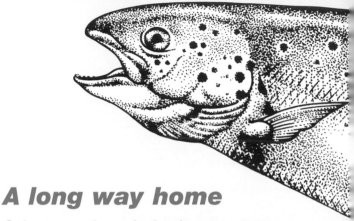

A long way home

Salmon are born in freshwater streams and rivers but live most of their lives in the sea. Eventually, they return to the place they were born to lay eggs. This can mean a journey of more than 2,000 miles (3,200 km) for some salmon. Many have to swim against the current of mountain rapids and waterfalls to get back to their birthplace.

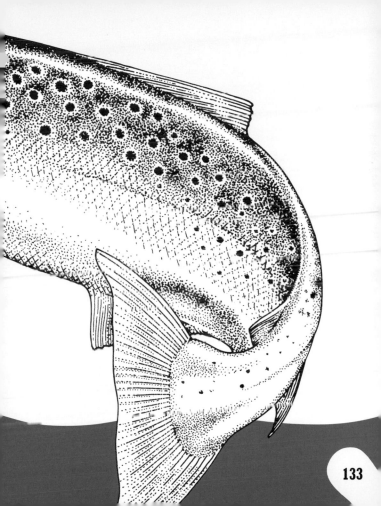

Hot wings

Many insects have to flap their wings very quickly to keep themselves in the air. This creates a lot of heat in the insect's body. Bumblebees reach a temperature of 104°F (40°C) while they are flying. A human would be very sick at that temperature.

Long distance traveler

Some gray whales make a round trip of 12,500 miles (20,000 km) each year. They follow food from the poles to the tropics.

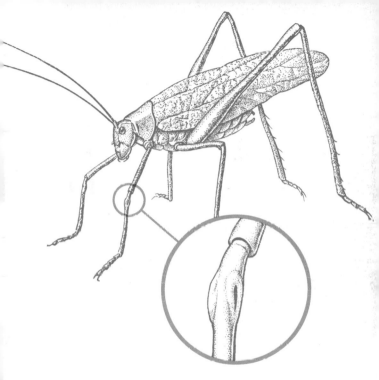

Sensing **sound**

Crickets communicate by
sound, which means they need
really good ears. Their sensitive
ears are found on their knees.

Sea spider

Sea spiders have between eight and twelve legs and are not related to the spiders that live on land. Some sea spiders are about 20 inches (82 cm) across.

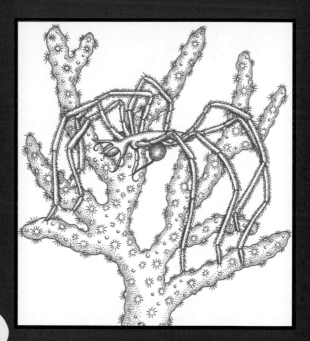

Fine feelers

Spiders' legs are very hairy. Each of these hairs is very sensitive. A spider can feel the slightest movement in its web through these hairs.

Echidna kids

Echidnas are a very rare kind of mammal that lays eggs. They keep their eggs in a pouch, a bit like a kangaroo's, until they have hatched and the young are ready to leave.

Skin-eaters in your bed!

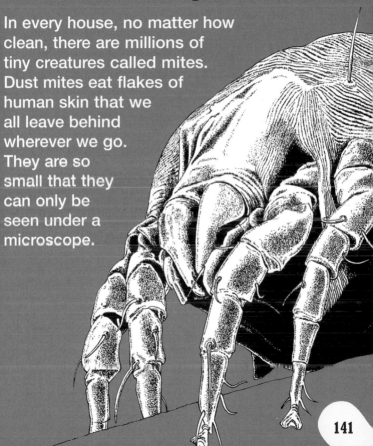

In every house, no matter how clean, there are millions of tiny creatures called mites. Dust mites eat flakes of human skin that we all leave behind wherever we go. They are so small that they can only be seen under a microscope.

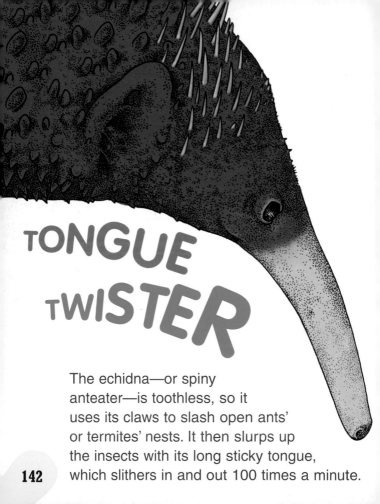

TONGUE TWISTER

The echidna—or spiny anteater—is toothless, so it uses its claws to slash open ants' or termites' nests. It then slurps up the insects with its long sticky tongue, which slithers in and out 100 times a minute.

MMM YUMMY!

The mantis is an insect that preys on other insects. The female will sometimes devour her own partner during mating, but the male can continue mating with her, even after his brains and head have been eaten!

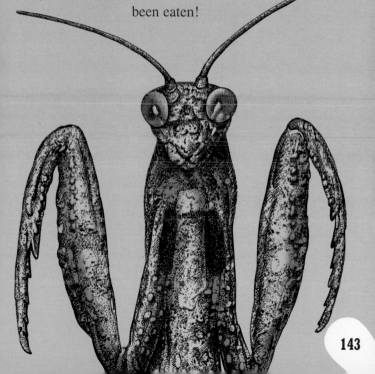

Land or sea

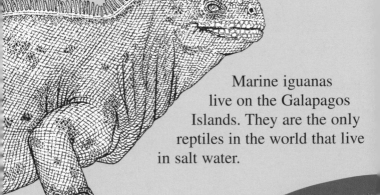

Marine iguanas live on the Galapagos Islands. They are the only reptiles in the world that live in salt water.

Stinging tale

Scorpions were some of the first animals in the world to live on the land. They have been around for about 440 million years.

Land iguanas, which
never go near the sea, also
live on the Galapagos
Islands.

145

Advancing *from the rear*

A Canadian porcupine has over 30,000 quills on its body. If it is attacked, it backs into its enemy, pushing its needle-sharp quills in. It then walks away, leaving a few quills behind.

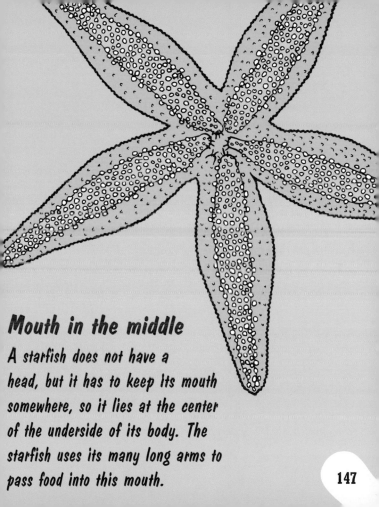

Mouth in the middle

A starfish does not have a
head, but it has to keep its mouth
somewhere, so it lies at the center
of the underside of its body. The
starfish uses its many long arms to
pass food into this mouth.

147

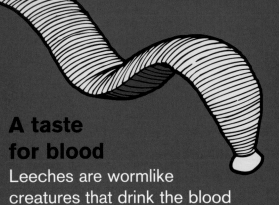

A taste for blood

Leeches are wormlike creatures that drink the blood of other animals. When they bite they inject a painkiller into the wound. The victim does not even notice that it has been bitten, so the leech can drink as much blood as it wants.

Tasting the air

The komodo dragon doesn't smell through its nostrils—it uses its tongue. It flicks its tongue out then presses it to the roof of its mouth where a special organ senses chemicals on it from the air.

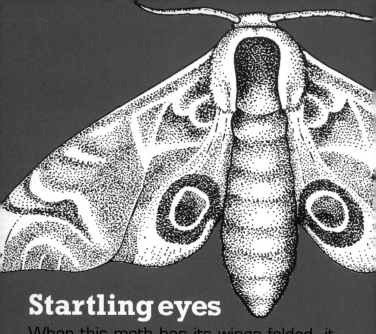

Startling eyes

When this moth has its wings folded, it
looks like a piece of old bark. If a bird
approaches, the moth opens its wings
and shows two spots that look like eyes.
The startled bird is likely to fly off
without trying to peck at the moth.

Night birth

Most foals are born at night. This is because, in the wild, the night is the only time a herd of horses would stay in one place for long.

Handwalking

Skunks get rid of attackers by turning their backs, standing on their front legs, and spraying the enemy with a really foul-smelling liquid.

Flying fish

Flying fish beat their fins from side to side and leap out of the sea at 35 mph (56 kph) They spread their side fins and glide through the air to escape from fish that are chasing them.

153

Magic uses of bats

Wash your face in bat's blood so that you can see in the dark.

Keep a bat bone in your clothes to give you good luck.

Use a powdered bat's heart to stop bleeding or deflect bullets.

Keep the right eye of a bat in your pocket to make you invisible.

Bad-luck bats

Bats have been linked to bad luck, evil, and witchcraft for thousands of years. This is probably because they mostly come out at night and fly around in silence.

A cackle of hyenas

Hyenas hunt at night in packs of about 30. They can run down large animals, which they attack with their sharp teeth. Their usual call is a long howl, but when excited they make a cackling noise.

Floating **food**

Aphids arc so small and light that thc wind can blow them miles (km) up into the air. Aphids and other tiny insects carried around in the air are sometimes called aerial plankton, because they are like the tiny creatures that float in the sea.

Built for speed

Marlins are very fast swimmers. They have extremely powerful muscles and their bodies are smooth and streamlined like jet fighters. Marlins can reach 75 mph (120 kph).

Web-footed dog

Labradors are very popular pets because they are intelligent and gentle. They also have webbed feet, just like ducks. This makes them very good swimmers.

Fossil *flatulence*

Many amber fossils contain ancient creatures, such as small insects and spiders, which were trapped and preserved in sap that then hardened into the amber. Some amber even contains gas bubbles emitted by the creatures. These time capsules of ancient farts enable scientists to discover the creatures' diets of 30 million years ago!

A lot of guts

Sea cucumbers use a disgusting
trick when they are under attack.
When a creature is trying to eat them
they squirt their guts out and swim away.
The predator eats the guts, and the
sea cucumber grows replacements!

BIG BUG

The world's biggest bugs live in tropical rainforests.

The goliath beetle of Africa grows up to four inches (10 cm) long and can weigh 3.5 ounces (1 kg).

Portuguese man-of-war

The Portuguese man-of-war is a jellyfish with tentacles that grow to 65 feet (19.8 m) long. These tentacles are covered with spines that shoot poison into anything that touches them. The poison kills fish and is very painful to people.

Blindfold bat

A bat can fly around without bumping into anything even if it is blindfolded. This is because it uses its ears to navigate. It makes squeaking noises and picks up the echoes as they bounce off objects ahead.

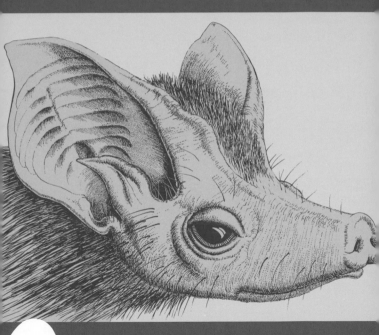

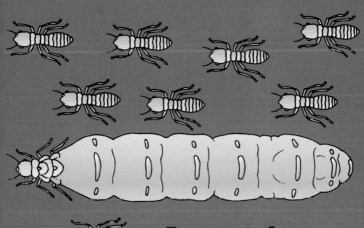

Busy mother

A termite queen spends her whole life in the nest, laying eggs. She is fed by worker termites a hundred times smaller than she is. The queen lays as many as 1,000 eggs a day.

165

Big bad wolf?

Buffalos are so big and strong that they can easily fight off a hungry wolf and are not really scared of them. Native Americans used to make themselves smell like wolves by wearing clothes made of wolf skin. That way they could get close enough to the buffalo to hunt them without scaring them away.

Sniffing beaks

Kiwis hunt for food at night using their excellent sense of smell. Unlike most birds, their noses are at the tip rather than the base of their beaks.

Elephant ears

Elephants have the biggest ear flaps of any animal in the world. An African elephant's ears are about 6 feet (1.8 m) across and are larger than an Indian elephant's. Elephants flap their ears to keep themselves cool.

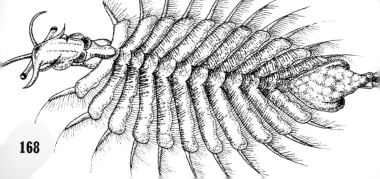

168

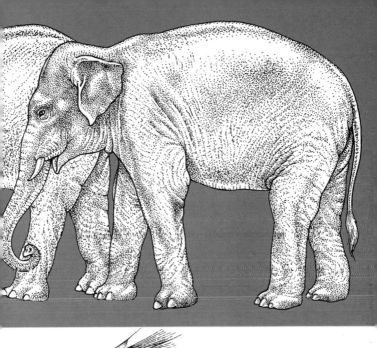

On its back

*The tiny brine shrimp swims along
upside down, moving its little legs
like the oars of a rowing boat.*

Sea cows

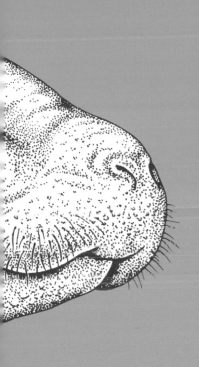

Manatees and dugongs are shy and gentle plant-eaters. They are the only mammals living in the sea that are completely vegetarian. They have big, grinding teeth, like elephants and cows, and only live in warm coastal waters.

171

Helpful hands

A shrimp has
nineteen pairs of arms
or legs. It uses two pairs
to find food in the water, one pair as
jaws, five pairs to handle its food, five
pairs to walk with, five pairs to swim
and breed, and the last pair as a tail.

Big bite

Hippos do not look like
dangerous animals,
but a fully-grown
hippopotamus can
bite a crocodile in
half with its huge
and powerful jaws.

172

Sick as a fly

When a housefly has finished its meal, it flies off and vomits its food. Then it eats it again. The dirty spots you see on windows are flies' vomit, which often carries germs that can spread disease.

One is better than none

The *Amoeba proteus* is a creature with just one cell. Human beings are made up of trillions of cells. Even though it is so simple, it can still move around and sense its surroundings.

176

Returning
home

Some swallows are born in Alaska and then fly all the way to Argentina for the winter. Later, they fly all the way back to Alaska to lay eggs.

Soaring

The Andean condor has huge wings that are perfect for soaring. It takes advantage of rising air warmed by the Sun to stay in flight. In this way it hardly ever has to flap its wings, so it can stay in the air for a long time with very little effort.

Camouflage

The sargassum fish and the sea dragon are very hard to find. Parts of their bodies look like the thick seaweed that they both live in.

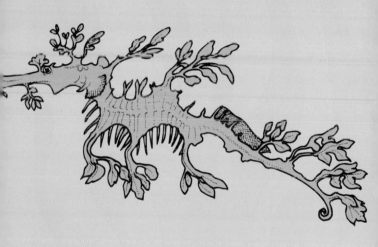

Optical **illusion**

Zebras' stripes help to
confuse lions and other animals that
prey on them. When lots
of zebras gather together it is hard to see
where one zebra ends and the next one
begins. It is also hard to see which way they
are likely to run.

Hunting machine

The Chinese, during the reign of Kublai Khan,
used lions on hunting expeditions.
They trained the big cats to
pursue and drag down
massive animals,
from wild bulls
to bears, and
to stay with
the kill until the
hunters arrived.

Spitting fish

Who would guess that a fish could shoot down insects to eat? The archerfish, which lives in the swampy mangroves of Southeast Asia, can do just this. It squirts water out of its mouth to knock insects into the river.

Sleeping your life away

Some animals sleep every day and night through the winter. Their hearts slow down so that they do not need food or water. Marmots can hibernate like this for nine months of the year.

Coral jungle

Corals look like plants, but they are really tiny animals. Millions of them live together to create a coral reef. They feed on bits of food floating in the water.

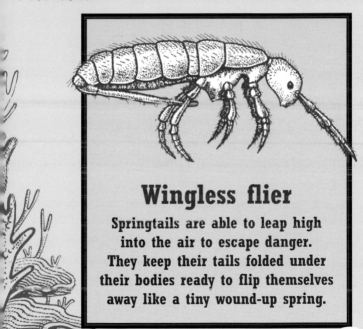

Wingless flier

Springtails are able to leap high into the air to escape danger. They keep their tails folded under their bodies ready to flip themselves away like a tiny wound-up spring.

FANGS A LOT!

Vampires are real! But they're not immortal gentlemen from Transylvania, they're bats. The vampire bat bites its victim with sharp teeth, then spends half an hour lapping up blood from the wound using its tongue. A vampire bat needs to eat about half its body weight in blood each day.

PLEASED TO
MEET YOU!

Deep in the tropical forest at night, the nocturnal slow loris crawls slowly and deliberately hand-over-hand along the branches searching for food. When it locates its prey it strikes with amazing speed. Gripping the branch with both back feet, it stands upright and throws itself forward seizing the creature with both hands.

BOING!!

One of the rarest animals in the world, the tarsier is so named because of its long tarsals (foot bones), which let it leap across gaps up to 20 feet (6 m) wide. This is 60 times its own body length.

A love dance

Courting sea eagles clasp each other's feet and twist and circle in the air.

A hopeful male often offers a female mouthfuls of fish as they race through the sky.

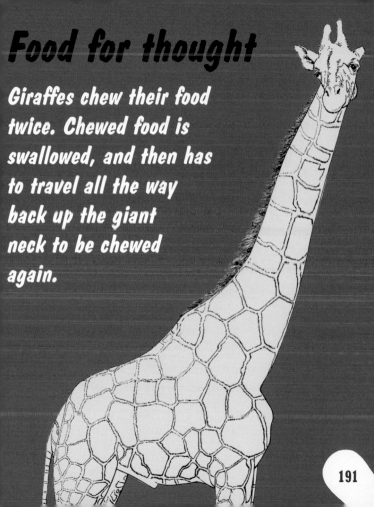

Food for thought

Giraffes chew their food twice. Chewed food is swallowed, and then has to travel all the way back up the giant neck to be chewed again.

Moth
facts

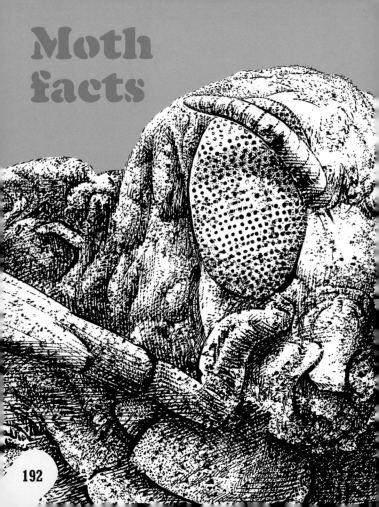

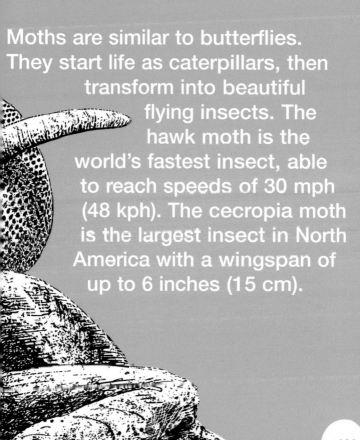

Moths are similar to butterflies. They start life as caterpillars, then transform into beautiful flying insects. The hawk moth is the world's fastest insect, able to reach speeds of 30 mph (48 kph). The cecropia moth is the largest insect in North America with a wingspan of up to 6 inches (15 cm).

Island poisoner

Solenodons are small, shrew-like animals that are found only on the islands of Cuba and Haiti. They have saliva that is poisonous to other animals but not to themselves.

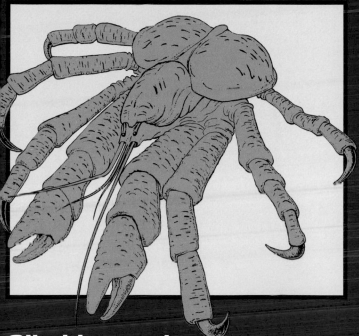

Climbing crabs

Spider crabs live on islands in the Pacific and Indian oceans. They grow to about 18 inches (45.7 cm) long and have very long legs, which they use to climb trees. When a crab gets to the top of a tree, it snips off a young coconut with its huge pincers and climbs down again to eat it.

Taking off

Flies have to beat their wings very quickly to stay in the air. The hover fly beats its wings 100 times per second when taking off.

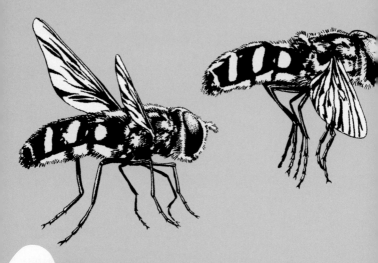

BURIED
ALIVE

The pink fairy armadillo is active at night. It generally moves very slowly but if it is threatened it can dig a burrow and completely bury itself within seconds. It then plugs the opening of the burrow using its flat rear armor plate like a cork.

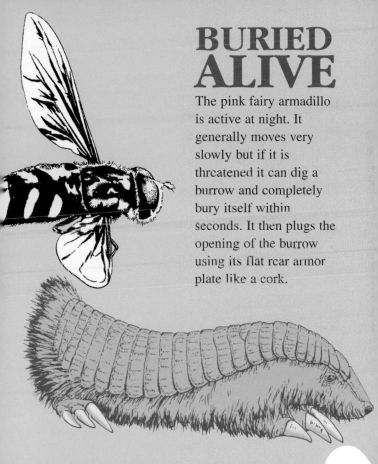

R-U-C-reus?

Koko the Gorilla lived in San Francisco zoo and was taught the same sign language used by deaf people. Koko could use more than 2,000 words, tell jokes, and even lie! When a scientist asked Koko if she were an animal or a gorilla, she replied, "Fine animal gorilla."

HELLO, I MUST BE GOING!

When frightened, the frilled lizard looks very scary. It raises its frill, opens its mouth wide and rears up on its hind legs. But if that is not enough to scare an enemy away, the lizard will turn and run up the nearest tree.

199

STEADY AS SHE GOES

Flies have two special organs called halteres that help them balance in flight. They look like two stalks with balls on the ends and are found just behind the wings. These flex as the fly changes direction and tell it the position of its body.

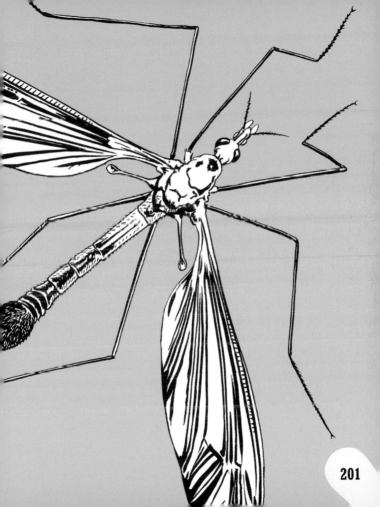

Outnumbered

There are more than 4,000 different types of mammal, including human beings. But there are more than 23,000 different types of fish.

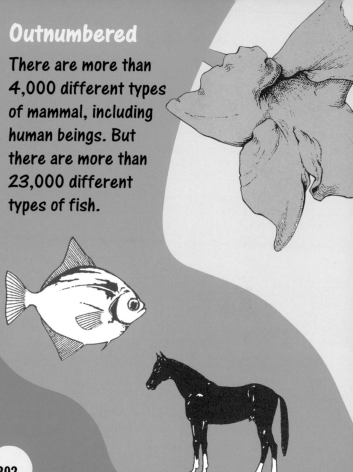

Feeding on the wing

Hummingbirds are tiny birds that feed on nectar from flowers. They can hover because they beat their wings very quickly. Their wings beat so fast that all you can see is a blur.

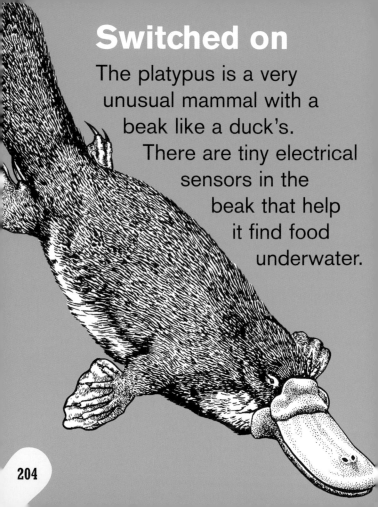

Switched on

The platypus is a very unusual mammal with a beak like a duck's. There are tiny electrical sensors in the beak that help it find food underwater.

204

Friendly foe

King Kong was a legendary giant gorilla that ate people. In fact real gorillas only eat fruit and vegetables.

A meal on a stick

Shrikes are very good fliers and
can catch insects in midair.
Sometimes they save a stack of
insects to eat later by pinning them
to a thorn or a small branch.

Flying lizard

The flying gecko
is one of several
animals that is able
to glide between
the treetops. It
has scaly fringes
along the sides of
its body, tail, and
webbed toes. These
act like a kind of
parachute if the
gecko needs to fall
a long way to the
ground.

A rat as big as a cat!

Tongue-tied

Pangolins are anteaters that live in Africa and southern Asia. They have no teeth and cannot chew, but have long, sticky tongues to collect ants to eat.

The biggest rodent of all, the capybara, is semi-aquatic and feeds on grasses near water. It is up to 24 inches (60 cm) high at the shoulder and weighs as much as 145 pounds (66 kg).

Furry bees

*A **bumblebee** has a coat made of furry scales. This keeps its body warm so that the muscles that beat its wings can work properly.*

READY TO GO

Jackrabbits are not actually rabbits at all, they are very fast-moving hares with powerful long hind legs. Like all hares, they do not build nests. The mother chooses a place she likes and the young are born there with their eyes wide open and ready to run.

FANCY A BITE?

Sometimes called "the man-eater" or "white death," the great white shark is one of the most deadly hunters in the sea. It has up to 600 teeth, which are as sharp as daggers. When one tooth wears out or is broken off, it is replaced by another.

Fastest creature

The spine–tailed swift from Asia is the fastest creature in the world. It has been recorded flying at a speed of 106.25 mph (171 kph).

Big burrower

Wombats are tough marsupials from Australia.
They like to dig long burrows—sometimes
almost 100 feet (33m) long—with their
powerful paws. Like other marsupials they
have a pouch for their young. Their pouches
face backward so they are not filled with
dirt while the wombat is digging.

215

It's the pits

Rattlesnakes and pit vipers have a sense that very few other animals have. They can detect body heat using pits on both sides of their heads. This sense allows them to find warm-blooded prey, even in the dark.

Short life

A mouse lives for only two to three years—on average human beings live 25 times longer.

Jawless sucker

The first fish did not have jaws.
Lampreys are among the last of
these early fish still surviving.
A lamprey's mouth is a large
round sucker with lots of
horny teeth around
the edge.

Bats catch and eat insects in midair. Some bats scoop up large insects in flight using their tail membrane.

Food can be picked out of the tail "pouch" and eaten as an in-flight meal.

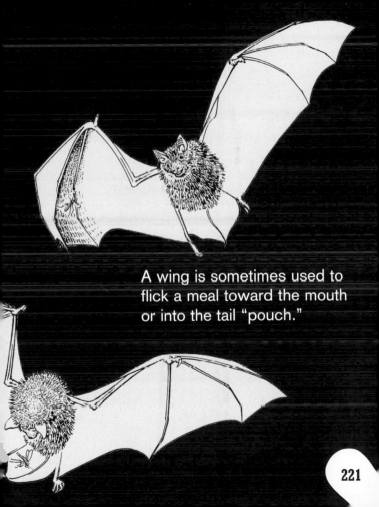

A wing is sometimes used to flick a meal toward the mouth or into the tail "pouch."

Ant herders

Some ants keep herds of aphids—tiny insects that live on plants—like people keep cows. The ants protect and look after the aphids. They "milk" them by stroking them with their antennae. The aphids then produce drops of clear liquid, which the ants like to eat.

Rhino horn

A rhinoceros's horn is made of the same stuff as hair and fingernails. The female rhino's front horn can grow to more than 5 feet (1.5 m)—that's at least three times longer than your arm! She uses her horn to dig up roots to eat and to protect her babies.

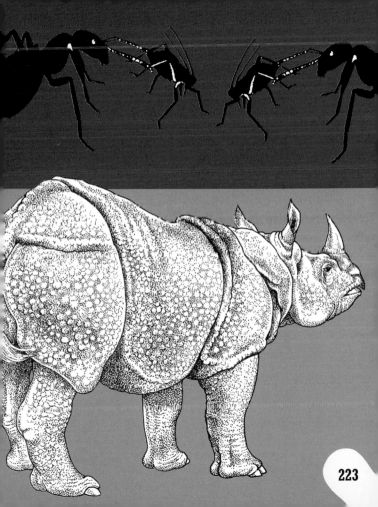

Bandicoot babies

The gestation period in some bandicoots—under 13 days—is the shortest of any mammal.

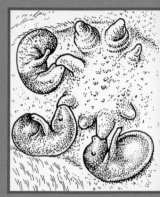

The baby crawls into the mother's pouch, which faces the rear.

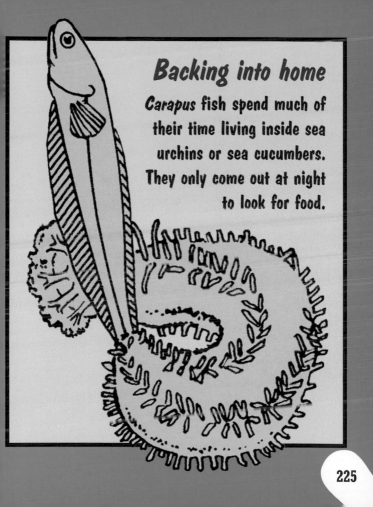

Backing into home

Carapus fish spend much of their time living inside sea urchins or sea cucumbers. They only come out at night to look for food.

Eyes alert

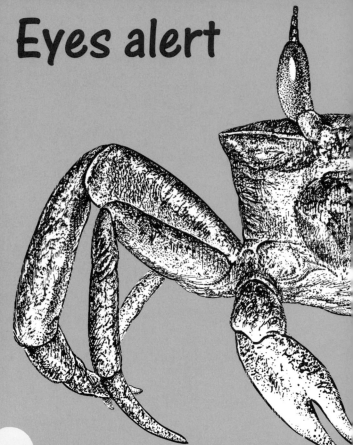

Crabs have lots of enemies, so they need to keep a sharp lookout. Their eyes are on stalks and each eye can look in different directions.

Sea squirt

The sea squirt looks more like a vegetable than an animal, but it has a heart, a stomach, and reproductive organs like other animals.

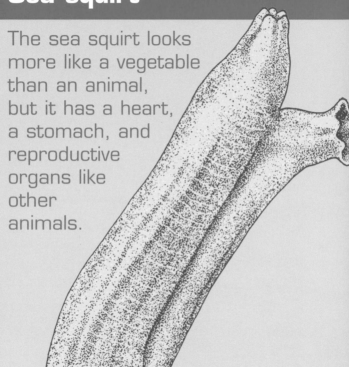

High pantry

After a leopard has eaten as much of a kill as it can, it drags the remains up a tree and hangs it on a branch for later. The stored food is safe from jackals and hyenas there.

Breathing through your stomach

Crickets breathe through their stomachs. They get oxygen from the air through lines of small holes along the sides of their bodies. Other insects also have these breathing holes which are called spiracles.

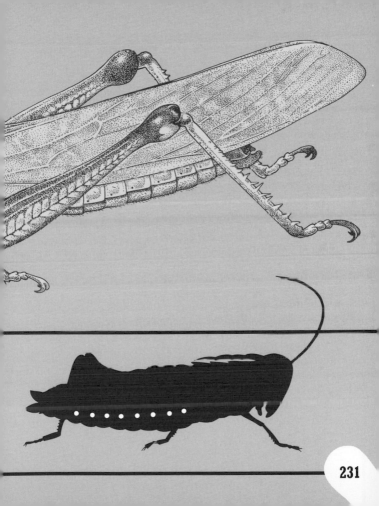

Hello buddy

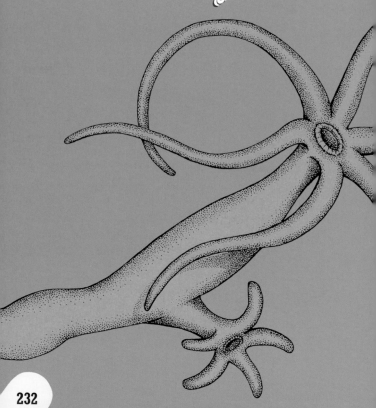

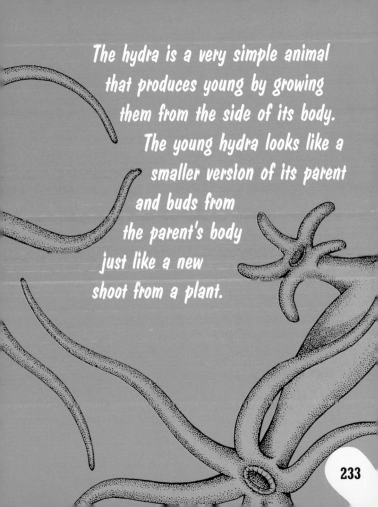

The hydra is a very simple animal that produces young by growing them from the side of its body. The young hydra looks like a smaller version of its parent and buds from the parent's body just like a new shoot from a plant.

THE **EYES** HAVE IT

An animal that hunts usually has eyes at the front of its head. This allows it to spot and follow prey. Animals that are hunted often have eyes on the sides of their head. This allows them to see all around them and spot approaching enemies early. Some spiders have more than two eyes looking in the same direction.

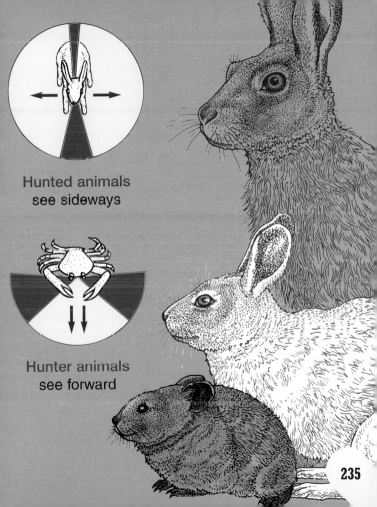

Hunted animals
see sideways

Hunter animals
see forward

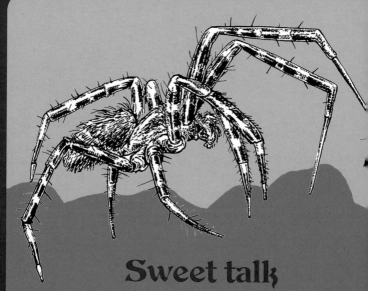

Sweet talk

Male spiders have to be very
careful about how they
communicate with female spiders.
If they get it slightly wrong, the
female is likely to mistake the male
for prey and eat him.

Sidewinder

The sidewinder is a snake
that lives in very hot deserts.
The sand is so hot that
the snake moves by
wriggling sideways
so that its
body only
ever touches
the ground at
two points.

Night light

*Male glowworms can fly like other
beetles, but the female cannot. She
has a glowing light on the end of her
body so that the male can find her in
the long grass at night.*

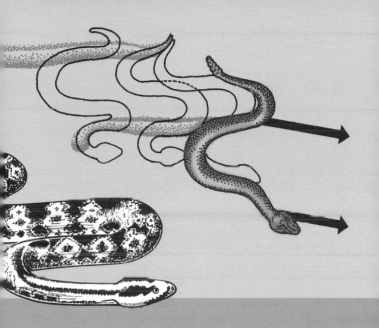

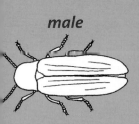

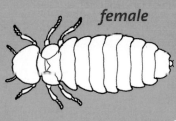

male

female

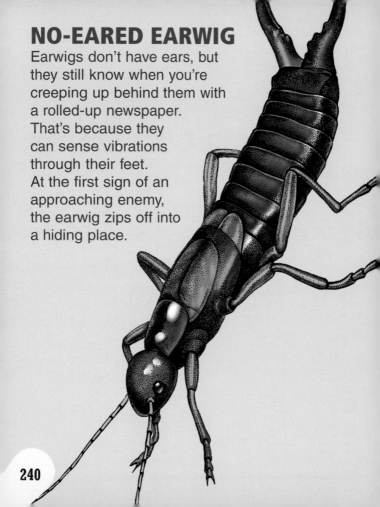

NO-EARED EARWIG

Earwigs don't have ears, but
they still know when you're
creeping up behind them with
a rolled-up newspaper.
That's because they
can sense vibrations
through their feet.
At the first sign of an
approaching enemy,
the earwig zips off into
a hiding place.

240

BIRDS WITH
TEETH
Members of the
crocodile family
are reptiles
related to birds.

MOUTHFUL
The pufferfish looks like a
perfectly ordinary fish
and lots of bigger
fish probably
think it looks
quite tasty too, until
they get too close. When it gets scared, the
pufferfish quickly swallows lots of water and
swells up into a prickly ball twice its normal
size. Even hungry predators think twice
before trying to take a bite out of something
that looks like a spiky cannon ball!

SMALL *BUT DEADLY*

Viruses are extremely small and simple. They are so simple that some scientists don't believe that they can even be said to be alive. As a comparison, the weight of a virus compared to a human being is about the same as the weight of a human being compared to the entire Earth.

LEAPS AND BOUNDS

Red kangaroos from Australia can jump more than 39 feet (12 m) in a single bound. When they are racing along at top speed they can reach 40 miles per hour (64 kph).

A mother kangaroo carries her baby in a stomach pouch.

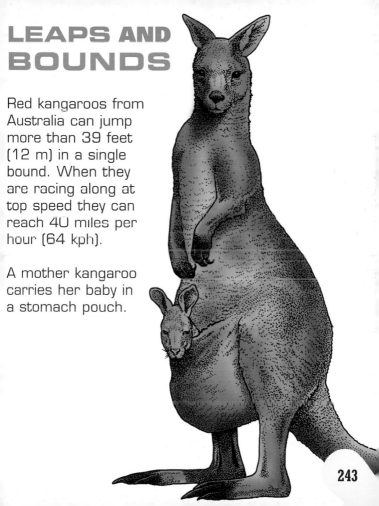

PLANT ANIMALS

Some creatures that live in the sea, such as sponges or *Obelia*, look more like plants than animals. These creatures usually stay in one place and catch food that floats by with their waving arms.

AMAZING **ANTS**

An ant can lift fifty times its own weight. If an ordinary man could do the same, he would be able to lift 8,100 pounds (3,675 kg). That's the weight of two automobiles!

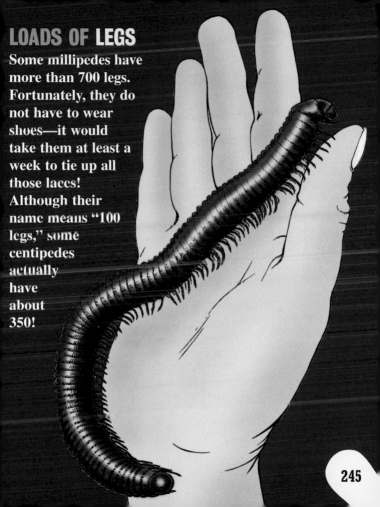

LOADS OF LEGS

Some millipedes have more than 700 legs. Fortunately, they do not have to wear shoes—it would take them at least a week to tie up all those laces! Although their name means "100 legs," some centipedes actually have about 350!

BRAVE DENTIST

Animals sometimes help each other out. The plover lives in Egypt and likes to pick bits of food out of crocodiles' mouths. The crocodile gets nice clean teeth, and the plover gets to eat anything it finds.

TERMITE TOWERS

Termites are insects that look like ants. They build huge towers to live in what are known as termite mounds. The largest termite mound ever found was more than 40 feet (12 m) tall—that's more than 2,000 times taller than a termite. If humans built towers that tall, they would be almost 11,480 feet (3,500m) high! In fact, the tallest building built by humans is only 1,671 feet (509 m) high.

DON'T BEE-LIEVE YOUR EYES

The hover fly has the same black and yellow stripes as a bumblebee, but it has no sting. The clever hover fly tricks its enemies into thinking they might get stung by looking like a bee.

247

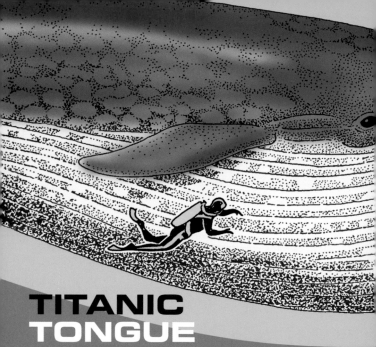

TITANIC
TONGUE

The blue whale is the biggest animal that has ever lived on Earth, but it lives on the smallest animals—tiny creatures called krill.

A whale uses special filters in its mouth to strain the krill out of the water, then shovels them down its throat using a tongue that weighs four tons. Krill are so small that a blue whale needs to eat about four million of them a day to stop its stomach rumbling!

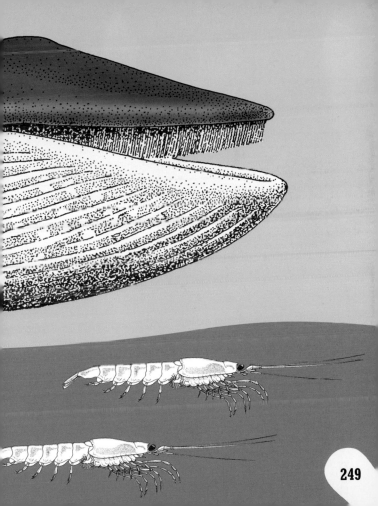

A CRACKING STORY

The crossbill is the only bird whose beak crosses over from either the right or left. It uses this beak to extract seeds from pine cones, and can eat 3,000 of them per day!

CLAM **UP**!

Some giant clams have shells that are more than 3 feet (1 m) wide and weigh 400 pounds (200 kg). It wouldn't be easy to bring one of those back from the beach!

THAT'S **COOL**

The Arctic fox lives further north than any other fox. It has the warmest fur of any mammal, even warmer than the polar bear. This means it can sleep on the surface of snow at an astonishing -58°F (-50°C).

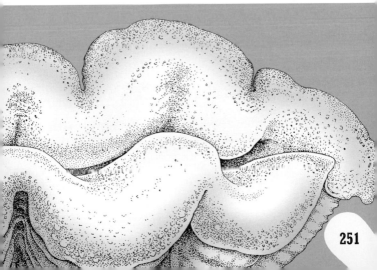

WHAT'S THE POINT?

The babirusa, an Indonesian wild pig, has huge sharp tusks growing from its mouth. These don't do the pig any favors though: if they head-butt with them, the tusks just point straight back into their own heads.

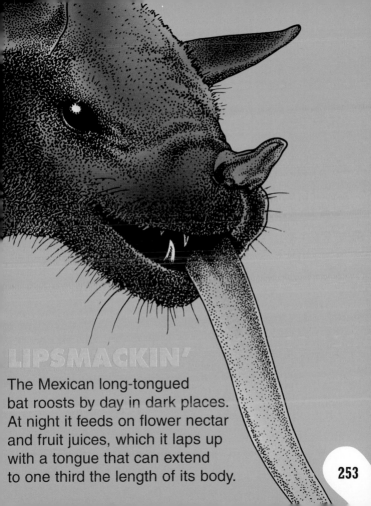

LIPSMACKIN'

The Mexican long-tongued
bat roosts by day in dark places.
At night it feeds on flower nectar
and fruit juices, which it laps up
with a tongue that can extend
to one third the length of its body.

White lie

Polar bears are not really white. Their fur is
actually clear, like glass, and each hair is hollow.
Air gets trapped inside the hairs helping to keep
the bear warm. Polar bears look white because
all those clear hairs together create
an optical illusion.

INSECT ID

Most people think that spiders are insects. In fact they are arachnids. Arachnids have bodies with two parts and eight legs, while insects have bodies with three parts and six legs. Scorpions, mites, and ticks are also arachnids.

STILL *SWIMMING*

The coelacanth (pronounced see-la-kanth) is a very old fish indeed. Scientists found fossils of coelacanths that were about 60 million years old and assumed the fish was extinct. They were very surprised when a fisherman caught a living coelacanth in the Indian Ocean. Who knows what other "extinct" creatures are still alive somewhere?

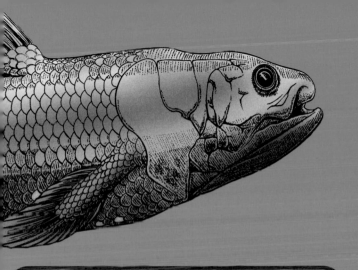

SNAIL'S PACE

The fastest snails in the world can move 328 feet (100 m) in about two hours. A human athlete can run the same distance in less than ten seconds, but not if he is carrying his house on his back!

ENORMOUS EGGS

Ostriches lay huge eggs. An ordinary ostrich egg is usually about 25 times bigger than a chicken's egg. One ostrich on a farm in China laid an egg that weighed 5 pounds (2.35 kg). The shell of an ostrich egg is so strong that a person can stand on it without breaking it. Don't try that with your boiled egg in the morning!

BIG CROC

Saltwater crocodiles living in northern Australia often grow up to 20 feet (6 m) long.

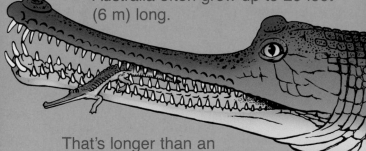

That's longer than an automobile, so you can't keep a crocodile in your garage!

FLYING FISH

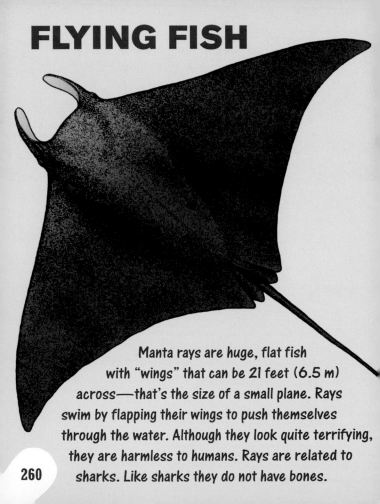

Manta rays are huge, flat fish
with "wings" that can be 21 feet (6.5 m)
across—that's the size of a small plane. Rays
swim by flapping their wings to push themselves
through the water. Although they look quite terrifying,
they are harmless to humans. Rays are related to
sharks. Like sharks they do not have bones.

MULTICOLORED MARVEL

Chameleons are perhaps the weirdest creatures in the world. They can change the color of their skin to blend in with the background and they've got rotating eyes that can point in opposite directions. They also have an extremely long tongue with a sticky end which they can shoot out and trap bugs with.

PINK PLUMAGE

Flamingos are famous for their pink plumage. The color comes from their food. They eat shrimps and tiny water plants that contain an orange substance called carotene. If a flamingo eats other food, its feathers slowly turn gray.

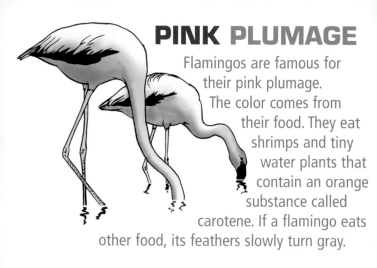

KEEP *MOVING*

Most fish have swim bladders (a bit like water wings) that keep them afloat, even when they are not swimming. Sharks do not have swim bladders. They have to keep moving all the time or they would sink. Sharks cannot swim backward either, unlike most other fish.

HEAVY HOUSE

The giant tortoise is famous for being a slow beast. A giant tortoise's shell weighs about 440 pounds (200 kg)—at least twice the weight of an average man—and the poor old tortoise has to carry it for all 150 years of its life. No wonder they don't rush around!

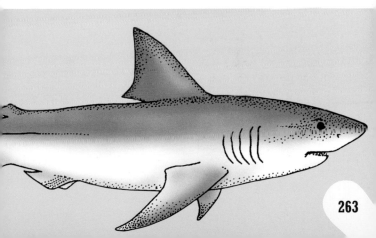

SLOW SLOTH

The three-toed sloth is probably the world's laziest animal. On the ground it moves at a maximum speed of 6 feet (1.8 m) a minute. Most of the time it lives in the trees, where it sleeps for 18 hours each day.

FEARSOME FISH

Piranha fish are famous for being small but dangerous flesheaters. A piranha has very sharp teeth and is attracted to the smell of blood in the water. A group of piranha fish can strip all the meat from a large animal such as a horse in a few minutes.

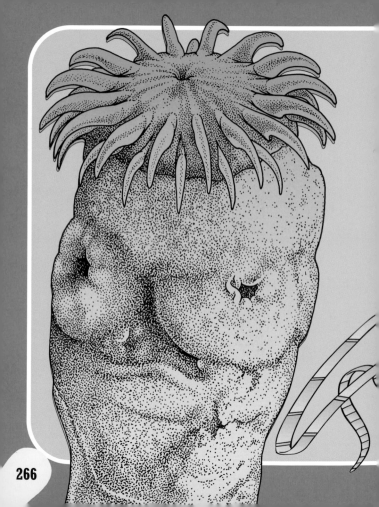

HOOK HEAD

The tapeworm lives inside the intestines of other animals—including humans! It uses the hooks in its head to anchor itself in place.

Some grow to 50 feet (15 m) long. That's more than three quarters the length of a tenpin bowling lane. They possess both male and female sex organs, so they do not need a mate to reproduce.

Dancing bees

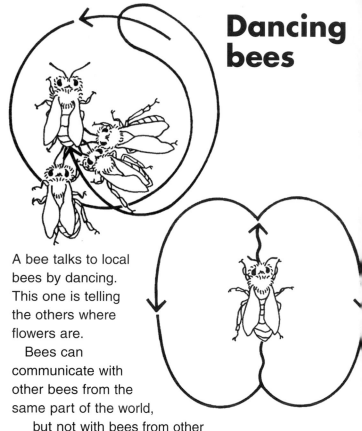

A bee talks to local bees by dancing. This one is telling the others where flowers are.

Bees can communicate with other bees from the same part of the world, but not with bees from other places. A French bee would not be able to understand an American bee.

COUNTING SHEEP

There are many superstitions about sheep.
One strange belief says that it is impossible to count
the number of sheep in a flock unless you have
washed your eyes in running water.

WORLD-WIDE WEB

Spiders are strange and mysterious creatures that have the ability to weave webs. All over the world, they have always been seen as magical because of this. Killing a spider is thought to bring bad luck. Walking into a spider's web is supposed to mean that you will soon meet a friend.

QUICK
EARS

Cats have 32 muscles that control the position of each ear—humans only have six. Cats' ears can quickly swivel to locate the direction a sound is coming from.

271

BUGS *WEIGH IN TOP*

If you collected all the insects in the world and put them on a huge set of scales with all the other creatures in the world (including people) on the other side, the insects would weigh more.

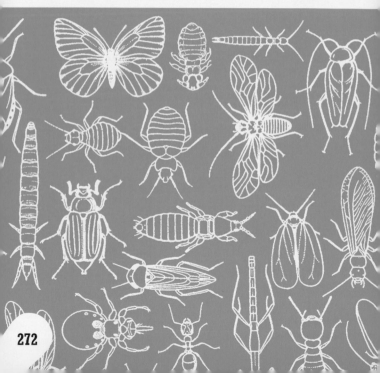

Lucky donkey

In the Bible, Jesus rode a donkey into
Jerusalem and was greeted as a savior.
People used to believe that the dark
markings on a donkey's back began on that
day. Because of this, black hairs from a
donkey's back were thought to cure
illnesses and bring good luck.

273

SEEKING A PARTNER

Female moths release particular chemicals that are detected by the featherlike antennae of the male. They can detect a female moth over 4 miles (6.4 km) away!

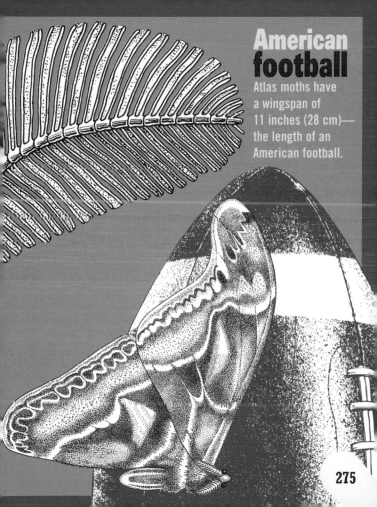

American football

Atlas moths have a wingspan of 11 inches (28 cm)— the length of an American football.

BEES NEVER TELL LIES

Honey bees have been regarded as wise and good creatures for thousands of years. This is especially true of bees kept in hives and raised for their honey. Many people believed that the hive had to be told when any important event happened in the life of the family that kept them.

ALBATROSS FORECAST

Sailors believe that the albatross is a sign of bad luck. In the days of sailing ships, an albatross seen circling a ship at sea was thought to mean that bad weather was on the way.

It was also considered extremely bad luck to kill an albatross.

277

PERFECT PITCH

An owl can detect its prey by using its ears. The facial ring of feathers helps to channel sound into its sensitive ears. It can detect, locate, and attack its prey in total darkness.

TUNNEL VISION

An owl's eyeballs are shaped like tubes. It cannot move its eyes to look at something: it has to move its whole head.

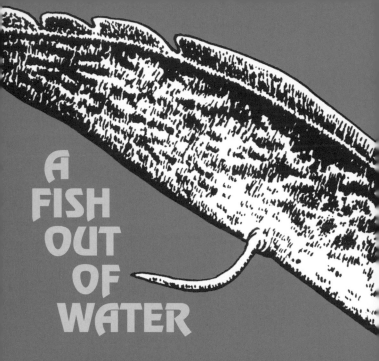

A FISH OUT OF WATER

The African lungfish is a very strange kind of fish. It can survive on dry land for up to four years, cocooning itself in a burrow in times of drought.

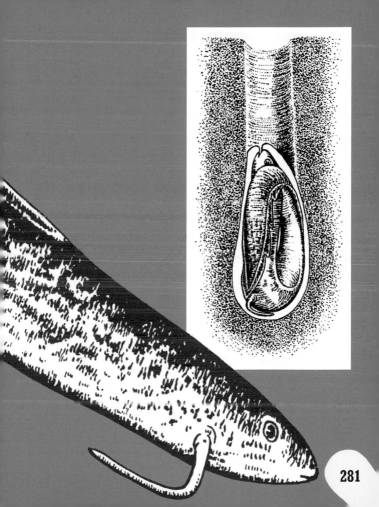

281

Counting
feathers

The highest known feather count was on a swan that had 25,216—more than 20,000 of which were on its head and neck.

Each wing area of a white swan is about 525 square inches (3,400 cm²), shown here against a man's arm at a comparable scale.

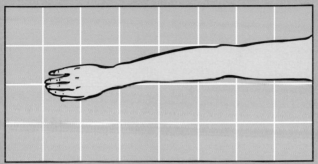

Swan song

The elegant swan has inspired many superstitions. It used to be said that when a swan dies it sings a beautiful melody. This is where the expression "swan song" comes from.

SNAKES' SENSE

Snakes cannot be harmed by their own poison. But snakes do not know this, so they are very careful not to bite their own tongues.

RAT TALES

Rats are able to eat just about anything, including other rats. But they cannot throw up! You are less likely to be bitten by a rat than your average-sized family pet dog. Rats cannot see very well. Sometimes they weave their heads from side to side when they are trying to get a good look at something: the movement gives them a better idea of what they are looking at.

INDEX

aardvarks 72
albatrosses 31, 277
amebas 176
ants 222, 244
aphids 157, 222
archerfish 184
armadillos 197
axolotl 126
babirusas 252
bacteria 12
bandicoots 224
bats 154, 155, 164, 220
    long-tongued 253
    vampire 188
bears, polar 254
beavers 80
bees 78, 96, 268, 276
    bumblebee 134, 210
beetles, goliath 162
bellbirds 60
birds 37, 98
    fruit-eating 19
buffaloes 166
bushbabies 61
butterflies, monarch 70
camels 107
    Bactrian 59
    dromedary 59
capybaras 208
Carapus 225
cats 33, 42, 106, 271
centipedes 245
chameleons 261
clams, giant 250
cockroaches 24, 54

coelacanths 256
condors 178
corals 186
crabs 226, 234
    fiddler 32
    horsehoe 115
    spider 94
    tree 195
crickets 137, 230
    Sri Lankan 100
crocodiles 241, 246, 258
crossbills 250
cuttlefish 105
Diaphus 74
dogs 22, 42, 159
donkeys 273
dragonfish 76
dugongs 170
Dunkleosteus 82
eagles 90
earthworms, giant 108
earwigs 240
echidnas 140, 142
eels, garden 28
elephants 46, 168
feathertails 123
fish 202
flamingoes 262
fleas 99, 104
flies 20, 174, 200
flying fish 153
flying foxes 48
foxes, Arctic 251
frogs, poison-arrow 45
    tree 29
fulmars 88
geckos 121, 207
gerenuks 50